P E R T H :   S C O T

PERTH: SCOTT'S FAIR CITY–

The Fair Maid of Perth
&
Sir Walter Scott

A CELEBRATION & GUIDED TOUR

Paul S. Philippou

with

Roben Antoniewicz and Rob Hands

TIPPERMUIR
· BOOKS LIMITED ·

Perth: Scott's Fair City -
The Fair Maid of Perth & Sir Walter Scott –
A Celebration & Guided Tour.
Copyright © Paul S. Philippou with Roben Antoniewicz
and Rob Hands 2018. All rights reserved.

This first edition published and copyright 2018 by
Tippermuir Books Ltd, Perth, Scotland.

mail@tippermuirbooks.co.uk

www.tippermuirbooks.co.uk

Project Support: Jean Hands, Matthew Mackie, and Steve Zajda.
Photography: Roben Antoniewicz.
Illustrations: Rob Hands.
Cover Design: Matthew Mackie.

ISBN: 978-0-9954623-4-2 (paperback).

A CIP catalogue record for this book is available from the British Library.

Text styling and artwork by Bernard Chandler [graffik], Glastonbury, England.
Text set in Caslon 540 Std 11pt on 14pt.
Printed and bound by CPI Group (UK) Ltd, Croydon, CR0 4YY.

'One of the most beautiful points of view which Britain, or perhaps the world, can afford, is, or rather we may say was, the prospect from a spot called the Wicks of Baiglie, being a species of niche at which the traveller arrived, after a long stage from Kinross, through a waste and uninteresting country, and from which, as forming a pass over the summit of a ridgy eminence which he had gradually surmounted, he beheld, stretching beneath him, the valley of the Tay, traversed by its ample and lordly stream; the town of Perth, with its two large meadows, or Inches, its steeples, and its towers; the hills of Moncrieff and Kinnoul faintly rising into picturesque rocks, partly clothed with woods; the rich margin of the river, studded with elegant mansions; and the distant view of the huge Grampian mountains, the northern screen of this exquisite landscape.'

The Fair Maid of Perth by Sir Walter Scott (1828)

'Scott's novels, which once were so popular they inspired "Scott mania" – from dances, to tourism and fashions – have now fallen out of favour, but at heart they remain rollicking reads.'

'You'll never see this on the BBC… the greatest Scottish novels NEVER adapted for TV.'
Vicky Allan, *Sunday Herald*, 24 December 2017

DEDICATION

To Sir Walter Scott for his part in
the development of the historical novel and
for providing masterpieces of the genre.

CONTENTS

SIR WALTER SCOTT

A Brief Biographical Sketch

THE OLD TOWN OF EDINBURGH has the privilege of claiming Walter Scott as its son. Scott was born there in 1771 to Anne Rutherford and Walter Scott, a lawyer. Sickness in his early years resulted in Scott being sent to his grandfather's farm in the Borders. There, Scott fell in love with Border history and culture. It was this love that bore the fruit of his interest in the ballads and folk traditions of Scotland.

After attending the High School in Edinburgh, Scott went on to study law at the university there, and in 1786 he was indentured in his father's legal practice. During this time, Scott was frequently sent on company business to the Perthshire Highlands. It is likely that these visits helped to internalise in the future bard a passion and empathy for the history, culture, and life of the Highlands. Throughout Scott's body of work the themes of Highland and Lowland life are played out. This is especially so in the poem *The Lady of the Lake* (1810), in *Waverley* (1814), the first in the series of novels internationally known as *The Waverley Novels*, and strikingly in *The Fair Maid of Perth* (1828).

Scott became an advocate in 1792, and Sheriff Depute of Selkirkshire in 1799. He married Charlotte Carpenter in 1797 and over the next few years Scott divided his time between Edinburgh, Selkirk, Lasswade, and later Ashestiel by the River Tweed. At this point in his life, Scott had produced a number of celebrated translations of German Romantic poetry; and had become known for his collections of Border ballads – his great

Left—Statue of Sir Walter Scott by the Cochrane Brothers (1845), South Inch.

three-volume *The Minstrelsy of the Scottish Border* (1802-3) appeared to great eulogy. Scott was also deeply influenced by and very much a part of Scotland's celebrated revival of philosophy and erudition, the 'Scottish Enlightenment', whose acclaimed leadership included Robert Burns, David Hume, Thomas Reid, and Adam Smith.

After appointment as Clerk to the Court of Session in 1806, Scott commuted between the Borders and Edinburgh. By 1812, he had accrued significant wealth, part of which he used to purchase a property that would see him become a Border laird, *Abbotsford*, near Melrose in the Scottish Borders. This 'conundrum castle' become Scott's life work but also a financial money pit. (The land upon which *Abbotsford* was built was originally *Cartly Hole Farm*, which Scott light-heartedly called *Clartyhole Farm*, after 'clarty' an expression used in Scotland and northern England for something unclean.) By 1826, *Abbotsford* had been transformed into a stately Border château. *Abbotsford* remained in the hands of Scott's descendants until recently, when the Abbotsford Trust took over the care and running of the house and estate with the addition of a new visitor centre.

Scott made his reputation as an internationally acclaimed poet, outstanding amongst his many poems being *The Lay of the Last Minstrel* (1805), *Marmion* (1808), the aforementioned *The Lady of the Lake* (1810), and *The Lord of the Isles* (1815). After being eclipsed as a poet by Lord Byron, Scott inclined his literary efforts to fiction.

The phenomenal success of *Waverley* (1814) was followed over the next eighteen years by twenty-seven novels, the collection installing Scott with the designations 'the world's best-selling novelist' and 'the pioneer of the historical novel'. The achievement of producing a novel every eight months without the benefit of modern technology and whilst maintaining a full-time job in the law is somewhat breathtaking. On average, Scott wrote some 4,000 words of finished text a day. *The Fair Maid of Perth* was, from start to finish, completed in four months.

Scott's work is recognised internationally as inspiration for many of the world's greatest novelists, from Leo Tolstoy, Honoré de Balzac, and Ivan Turgenev in Europe to Nathaniel Hawthorne and Fenimore Cooper in America. Moreover, Scott's influence on world writers was colossal. His sway nonetheless extended far beyond this. Scott presented strong views on nationalism, national identity, and a nation's culture at a time when Europe and the Americas were witnessing the birth of new and the expansion of existing nations. The great American writer Mark Twain made no secret of his dislike of the writings of Sir Walter Scott, he nonetheless testified, albeit satirically, that the American Civil War was seeded in Scott's novels.

Furthermore, Scott's stories had substantial attraction for Italian and German composers of operas. More than eighty operas have been composed from the *Waverley* novels, eleven of *Ivanhoe* (1820), eleven of *Kenilworth* (1821), five of *Guy Mannering* (1815), four of *Rob Roy* (1817), four of *The Heart of Midlothian* (1818), and seven of *The Bride of Lammermoor* (1819) – the most famous being Donizetti's *Lucia de Lammermoor* (1835). The long poems have also been adapted for opera: *The Lord of the Isles* inspired two Italian operas; *La Donna del Lago* (*The Lady of the Lake*) of 1819 launched Rossini's romantic period. *The Fair Maid of Perth* itself stimulated Bizet to pen *La jolie fille de Perth* (1867). It is said that the people of Perth were so taken with Bizet's efforts that the opera's libretto was sung around the city for decades after the opera was first performed.

Hollywood and television too has drawn inspiration from Scott with the online film database IMDB listing sixty-seven entries for Sir Walter Scott, including several productions of *Ivanhoe* (1913, 1952, 1982, and 1997), *Quentin Durward* (*c.*1956), *Rob Roy* (1922, 1995), and *Rob Roy, The Highland Rogue* (1953).

Many of Scott's novels, like *Waverley*, focus on Scottish history. He was fascinated by the periods of the theological and Covenanting wars in the seventeenth century, and the Jacobite risings of the eighteenth. Scott was particularly engrossed by times of disharmony and civil war in Scotland, *The Fair Maid of Perth* an example of this fascination. Set in the very late fourteenth century, the novel takes as its background the feuding between King Robert III and Scotland's unruly nobility. Alongside this turbulent national politic, Scott made use of the historical conflict between two bellicose Highland clans, Clan Kay and Clan Chattan.

The pre-eminent Scottish novels, written between 1814 and 1832, include *Waverley (1814), Guy Mannering (1815), The Antiquary* (1816), *Old Mortality* (1816), *Rob Roy (1817), The Heart of Midlothian (1818), The Bride of Lammermoor* (1819), *Redgauntlet* (1824), and *The Fair Maid of Perth* (1828). Scott however did not constrain himself to Scottish history. In addition to the seventeen volumes of Scottish historical fiction, Scott penned nine novels whose settings traverse the world stage, from *Ivanhoe* (1820) and *Kenilworth* set in England, *Quentin Durward* (1823) in France, *The Talisman* (1825) with the Crusaders in the Holy Land, *Anne of Geierstein* (1829) in Switzerland, and *Count Robert of Paris* (1832) in Constantinople – as well as a novella, *The Surgeon's Daughter* (1827), set in India.

In 1818, as Scott's career stood at its loftiness, he was made a baronet. Four years later, he played a major part in arranging the Royal Visit of George IV to Edinburgh. Scott saw this visit as something of a second coronation; and as the first time a reigning British monarch had come to Scotland for over 150 years, as a symbolic rapprochement after the Jacobite risings, and a reconciliation of the mutually mistrustful Lowlands and Highlands.

By the mid-1820s Scott was on top of his game; a celebrated poet and unequalled in acclaim as a writer with twenty-one novels under his belt. His latest great success that year was *The Talisman*, his majestic novel of the conflict between the Crusader king, Richard the Lionheart, and Saladin, the illustrious Muslim leader, together with his scholarly work as historian and editor of famous writers like Dryden and Swift. Amidst all this textual output, Scott found time to honour his legal involvements.

In 1826, Scott's life witnessed an abrupt rupture. Archibald

Constable, a great publishing house, with which through the firm of Ballantyne he had personal monetary investment, collapsed financially. Scott was bankrupt and in theory insolvent. Thankfully Scott's creditors agreed to allow him to pay what he owed out of future royalties on his books. A task Scott fully achieved before his death in 1832.

* * *

THE FAIR CITY OF PERTH

Its Etymology

IT IS GENERALLY CLAIMED that it is Sir Walter Scott who was responsible for Perth being designated '*The Fair City*'. Scott certainly enjoyed using the phrase in *The Fair Maid of Perth;* there being 108 occurrences of '*fair city*' within the novel. There is in addition some circumstantial evidence to suggest the veracity of the assertion of Scott's birthing of Perth as '*The Fair City*'.

The Scotsman, for example, for the period 1817 (when the newspaper was established) to 1828 (the year *The Fair Maid of Perth* was published) makes no use of the expression '*The Fair City of Perth*'; the same is true for *The Times* between the newspaper's founding in 1785 and 1828. After the publication of *The Fair Maid of Perth*, the term appeared in both newspapers, for example, in a piece entitled 'The Queen's Visit To Scotland' published in *The Times* on Saturday, 10 September 1842. On the other hand, the, *Statistical Accounts of Scotland*, 1791-1845, make no mention of Perth's '*Fair City*' epithet, either before or after 1828.

The most important archival evidence may be a letter (held in Perth & Kinross Archives) written to the Lord Provost of Perth of the time by the then Lord Advocate – Francis, later Lord Jeffrey, the Whig member for the Perth Burghs constituency – (December 1831) that refers to '*your fair city*'. As far as may be ascertained, there is no similar usage of the expression to be found prior to 1828 within the holdings of Perth & Kinross Archives. Significantly, there are, the aforementioned letter being but one example, several after that date.

Left—St John's Kirk, St John's Place.

THE FAIR MAID OF PERTH

Its Characters

CATHARINE GLOVER, a comely young woman of a pious religious nature, is the daughter of *Simon Glover*, widower, honest burgher, successful glove maker, and deacon of the Glover Incorporation of Perth. Her title, the *'Fair Maid of Perth'*, is an acknowledgement that she is the most beautiful of all the women of Perth and its district.

At the start of the novel, *Conachar*, later *Eachin (Hector) MacIan*, the Chief of Clan Quhele is apprenticed to *Simon Glover* and lives with *Simon*, *Catharine*, and their housekeeper *Dorothy* at their home in Curfew Street. Central to Scott's tale of romance is the brawny armourer, accomplished fighter, and maker of weapons, *Henry Gow*, known also as *'Hal o' the Wynd'*, the *'Gow Chrom'*, *'Harry Smith'*, *'Gobha Chrom'*, and comically, as the *'bent'*, that is *'the bandy legged smith of St Johnston'*.

Scott set his principal characters against a backdrop of royal intrigue bringing into the plot *King Robert III of Scotland*; his deceiving brother the *Duke of Albany*; the reckless and luckless *David, Duke of Rothesay*, the king's son and heir to the throne; the *Earl of March* and his jilted daughter *Elizabeth*; and the *Duchess of Rothesay*, daughter of the feared and renowned *Earl of Douglas*, known as the *'Black Douglas'*.

Oliver Proudfute (frivolous and boastful bonnet maker); his wife *Magdalen*; the scheming apothecary *Henbane Dwinning*; *Sir Patrick Charteris of Kinfauns* (Provost of Perth); *Sir John Ramorny of Fife* (Master of the Horse to the Duke of Rothesay); *Prior*

Left—Statue of the Fair Maid of Perth by Graham Ibbetson (1992), High Street.

Anselm (Prior of the Dominican friary); *Father Clement,* a free thinking Carthusian monk in dispute with the established church; and *Louise the glee maiden* (an entertainer from Provence) all feature in the story. So too do the minor characters *Bailie Craigdallie* (the city's most senior Bailie); the murderer *Anthony Bonthron* and *Eviot of Balhousie* (attendant and steward to *Sir John Ramorny,* respectively); the *Earl of Errol* (Lord High Constable of Perth); *Torquil of the Oak* (foster-father to *Conachar*); *MacGillie Chattanach* (Chief of Clan Chattan); *Gilchrist MacIan* (Chief of Clan Quhele and father of *Conachar*); *Stephen Smotherwell* (the executioner); *Father Francis* (a Dominican monk); the *Devil's Dick of Hellgarth* (kinsman of the '*Earl of Douglas*'); *Kitt Henshaw* (Agent to *Sir Patrick Charteris*); *Lindsey, the young Earl of Crawford*; *Sir Louis Lundin* (Town Council Clerk); *Niel Booshalloch,* an old friend of *Simon Glover*; and, *Norman-nan-ord, 'Norman of the Hammer'* (clansman of Clan Quhele).

* * *

THE FAIR MAID OF PERTH

A Synopsis

IT IS ST VALENTINE'S EVE, 1396. *Simon Glover, Catharine* his daughter, and *Conachar* his apprentice, attend mass at the Dominican friary close to their home in Curfew Street. At the church, a noble in disguise seeks to persuade *Catharine* to allow him to present himself at her window the next morning so that he may become her Valentine for the year. *Catharine's* refusal results in the nobleman's angry departure.

Henry Gow, who has just returned from a tour of Scotland selling armour (made at his smithy), calls upon the home of his friend *Simon Glover*. A meal is prepared by *Dorothy* the housekeeper. *Simon Glover* hopes for the marriage of *Catharine* to *Henry* but *Henry's* martial nature displeases *Catharine*.

Conachar and *Henry* quarrel after which the young Highlander draws his weapon and lunges at *Henry*. Easily dealt with by *Henry*, *Conachar* retires to his loft room. Although backed by *Catharine's* father, *Henry*, who loves the mild-mannered *Catharine*, appears too pugnacious to win her over. He is encouraged by *Simon Glover* to return early the next morning to secure *Catharine* as his Valentine.

The following morning, dressed in his finest garments but with the protection of his chainmail and a sword beneath his cloak, *Henry* makes his way to Curfew Street. As he arrives, he sees a group of courtiers (unbeknown to him the sovereign's son, the *Duke of Rothesay*, and men of his company) attempting to abduct *Catharine*. The kidnap is thwarted by the intervention of

Left—Fair Maid's House, North Port.

Henry who in the ensuing fight severs the hand of one man and briefly seizes another of the kidnappers. The amputated man is *Sir John Ramorny*, Master of Horse to the *Duke of Rothesay*. As the prospective kidnappers run off, the citizens of Perth take to the streets. *Oliver Proudfute*, a bonnet maker, holds the severed hand aloft.

Henry is invited into *Simon Glover's* home where he dozes off in a chair. As the sun rises the next day, *Catharine*, who has observed *Henry* in his slumber, kisses him on the lips. *Henry* awakes and soon *Catharine* is his Valentine for the year. This delights *Simon Glover. Conachar* is far from pleased and after taking breakfast abandons his apprenticeship to return home to the Highlands.

Early on St Valentine's Day, *King Robert* (III) is engaged in conversation with the *Duke of Albany* at the Dominican friary; *Prior Anselm* is in attendance. The *Earl of March* and his men arrive. So too does the *Earl of Douglas. Louise the glee maiden*, a courtesan and entertainer, makes an appearance and some trouble ensues. *Henry* is charged by *Rothesay* to escort the *glee maiden* to a place of safety. Against his own counsel, *Henry* agrees to *Rothesay's* request.

Henry and the *glee maiden* sneak out of the friary. *Henry*, unsure of what to do with the girl, eventually takes her to his home where she is placed in the charge of his *housekeeper.* En route to his house, the pair are spotted by *Dwinning* the apothecary. Meanwhile, *King Robert, March, Albany, Anselm*, and *Rothesay* discuss the incident in Curfew Street; the severed hand is produced. They also discuss the long-standing feud between Clan Chattan and Clan Quhele. It is agreed that the feud will be resolved by a judicial mortal combat between thirty members of each clan in the presence of the sovereign.

Dwinning attends *Ramorny* for the loss of his hand and shares with him his hatred of *Henry*. Revenge is plotted. Instructing his servant *Bonthron* to murder *Henry, Ramorny* hopes for revenge.

Morris dancers and revellers fill the streets of Perth. *Oliver*

Proudfute is caught up in the revelry. The scared bonnet maker makes his way to the home of *Henry*. *Proudfute* borrows *Henry's* buff-coat and cap of steel believing that mimicking the black-smith in gait and manner will keep him safe. He is however attacked as he makes his way to his own dwelling. A blow from behind ends his life. *Ramorny's* assassin has killed the wrong man.

Rothesay, accompanied by the revellers enter the home of *Ramorny*, who, having taken an opiate supplied by the apothecary, is indisposed. Undeterred by *Ramorny's* attendant *Eviot*, *Rothesay* gains entrance to *Ramorny's* bedchamber where he discovers it was he who lost his hand in the Curfew Street skirmish. *Eviot* receives instruction to bring *Bonthron* before *Rothesay*. *Bonthron* appears, bloodied with axe in hand, fresh from the murder of *Proudfute*.

Outraged by the murder of one of their own, the people of Perth assemble in the city's Council Chamber. *Henry* is called for but is reluctant to become involved having pledged martial temperance to his beloved *Catharine*.

No longer able to avoid the matter, *Henry* joins his kinfolk who through intelligence are aware of the involvement of *Ramorny's* household in the slaying of *Proudfute*. It is decided to use the ancient rule of 'Bier Right' – the ordeal of appearing before the corpse one is alleged to have slain; the bleeding of the corpse indicating guilt – to confront members of that household and thus find the killer.

Henry is appointed champion by *Proudfute's* widow. *Ramorny's* household appears before *King Robert* and his court at St John's Kirk. At the appointed moment *Bonthron* refuses to present himself to the corpse and instead chooses combat. Bested by *Henry*, *Bonthron* admits his guilt and accuses *Rothesay* of complicity. *Bonthron* is taken away to be hanged. With the aid of *Dwinning* and the executioner *Smotherwell*, *Bonthron* survives the hanging to be released from the scaffold and whisked away to Newburgh under cover of night.

In danger of accusations of heresy, *Catharine* and *Simon*

Glover receive the help of *Provost Charteris*. The three of them make their way to Kinfauns where *Catharine* remains whilst *Simon Glover* travels north-west to Loch Tay.

Reaching Bullough near Loch Tay, *Simon Glover* arrives at the home of *Niel Booshalloch*, an old friend who informs him of the death of *Gilchrist MacIan*, Chief of Clan Quhele, and the ascendency of *Conachar* to that title. The funeral of Clan Quhele's former captain is held at Loch Tay. From a nearby hill, *Simon Glover*, in the company of *Father Clement*, watches the Highlanders honour their chief. *Conachar*, now *Eachin (Hector) MacIan*, is inaugurated as clan chief on the banks of the loch. *Simon Glover* joins some 200 clan members at the celebratory banquet.

After the succession, *Simon Glover* spends some time as a guest of *Niel Booshalloch*. As the weeks go by, political developments offer fortune to *Catharine* and *Simon Glover's* predicament. *Father Clement* informs *Simon Glover* that the accusation of heresy brought by the High Court of Commission no longer stands.

At Perth, *Ramorny's* anger at the *Duke of Rothesay* spurs him to seek bloody vengeance. *Rothesay* is lured by the chance of frolics with *Catharine Glover* to accompany his old friend to the castle at Falkland, home of the *Duchess of Rothesay*. Taking a boat, *Ramorny*, *Rothesay*, *Dwinning*, and *Eviot* sail down the River Tay. During that journey the royal party meet another boat. *Rothesay* spies *Louise the glee maiden* on board and has her brought to his vessel.

At Newburgh, *Rothesay* and the others mount horses to complete the final part of the journey to Falkland. Unbeknown to *Catharine*, the *Duchess of Rothesay* is not at Falkland and the 'lady' whom she finds lying in her bedchamber is a disguised *Duke of Rothesay*. *Catharine* kisses the gloved hand of the person she believes to be the duchess. *Rothesay* places his arm around her and showers *Catharine* with kisses to which the *Fair Maid* reacts with revulsion. *Rothesay's* passion is calmed by *Catharine's* purity and nobility of words; he is contrite.

After taking dinner with *Ramorny* and *Dwinning*, *Rothesay*, drugged by the apothecary, is taken ill. After convincing the rest of the household that *Rothesay* has a contagious illness, the three conspirators, *Ramorny*, *Dwinning*, and *Bonthron*, take him by a secret staircase to a dungeon, wherein he is placed in irons and denied food. *Bonthron* acts as his warder.

The three conspirators are but pawns in the undertaking, for it is the *Duke of Albany* who has hatched the foul deed in pursuance of his and his family's designs on the throne. *Catharine* and the *glee maiden* imprisoned within the castle become close and *Catharine* learns the truth of how *Henry* assisted the *glee maiden's* escape from Perth.

The two women, whilst in the castle gardens, hear *Rothesay's* cries through a crack in the wall. Small amounts of food are passed to the prisoner through the crack. An escape plan is determined and executed successfully by the two women.

The *glee maiden* makes her way to the *Earl of Douglas* who marches upon the castle with a body of horse. His arrival is too late, for *Rothesay* is dead in his chamber; his lifeless body thrown on the bed in haste before his murderers could arrange his body to hide foul play.

The murderers are captured, hastily executed by hanging from the castle battlements, and then found guilty by a court of *Douglas's* men. Aware of *Albany's* role in the crime, *Douglas* decides it is politic to let the matter be left to 'God's Judgement'. Meanwhile, a bitter rivalry develops between *Henry* and *Conachar*, as both contend for *Catharine's* affections.

Henry fashions the best mail harness he has ever wrought, which *Norman-nan-ord* ('Norman of the Hammer') attempts to buy for *Conachar*. Hoping that providing *Conachar* with this protection will ensure his rival's survival in the clan combat and thus provide him with a chance at fighting *Conachar* himself, *Henry* agrees to the sale of the armour.

A couple of days before the judicial combat, the two clans march to Perth where they are kept separate. The people of

Perth are commanded not to approach within half a mile of the two camps. Clan Chattan bivouac at Kinfauns whilst Clan Quhele are billeted at the Abbey of Scone.

Shortly before the scheduled day and time of the battle, *Simon Glover* returns to Perth. He meets *Henry* on the North Inch. The two clans enter the specially built arena. Clan Chattan find themselves short of one fighter; the youngest of the clan.

Torquil attempts to save *Conachar* by offering to withdraw Clan Quhele's youngest fighter, their clan chief, from the combat. The plan fails and Clan Chattan seek a volunteer from the people of Perth with an offer of a gold crown. *Henry* relishes the opportunity of confronting *Conachar* and takes up the offer.

The battle begins and is bloody and terrible. The eight sons of *Torquil* perish one after the other in defence of their clan chief. *Torquil* too falls in defence of his 'Hector'. At the end of the conflict, *Henry* and *Conachar*, who is the only man of his clan still alive, face each other.

Fear overcomes *Conachar*, who flees by throwing himself into the River Tay and swimming to safety. At Campsie, *Conachar* meets *Catharine* who along with the *glee maiden* has been brought to stay with the *Duchess of Rothesay* under the order of the *Douglas*. Overcome with shame, *Conachar* confesses his failure to *Catharine* and throws himself into a raging cataract.

After the battle, *King Robert* learns of the death of his son. *Henry* offers a vow that in future he will only draw his sword to defend Scotland and is finally accepted by *Catharine* whom he marries.

* * *

THE EIGHT INCORPORATIONS
OF MEDIEVAL PERTH

AS EARLY AS THE Norman conquests of the eleventh century, artisans, craft workers, and merchants began to set up organisations (craft and merchant guilds) to control and regulate their commercial activity. It was these guilds that saw to the running of markets and fairs, and ensured the monarch received his or her due in taxes in line with the charters granted to them.

For Perth, the most famous such charter is that of William the Lion of Scotland – granted in 1210. Under this royal charter, the Burgh of Perth received authority to control trade within the city. Magistrates within royal burghs had the power to grant incorporation status to the guilds in effect providing them with a monopoly and protection from enterprises outwith the burgh.

The incorporations imposed rules and regulations controlling the quality of craftsmanship and entry to the profession. Each incorporation maintained a governing body comprising a deacon (master), boxmaster (treasurer), and a council of craftworkers. A court was held to uphold the incorporation's rules and for exercising discipline over their contravention.

The incorporations worked collectively and held the right to representation in the running of the burgh; a right maintained until its abolition by the Royal Burghs (Scotland) Act 1833 under which councils became electable bodies. The loss of their monopoly status in 1846 resulted in the incorporations being reduced to charitable bodies.

The eight incorporations of Perth were the bakers, fleshers, glovers, hammermen, shoemakers, tailors, weavers, and wrights.

Left—Edward VII Memorial (1913), King Edward Street.

SIR WALTER SCOTT & PERTHSHIRE

THE CITY OF PERTH and the towns and villages that make up its district have links with Scott as a visitor and as a novelist who drew upon their history and form. Known local associations with Scott include Invermay near Forteviot (to visit his first love Williamina Belsches of Fettercairn), Blairadam, Cleish, and of course, the *'Fair City of Perth'*.

Scott's local connections include his links with Lord Gray of Kinfauns and Grant of Kilgraston; and his close friendship with the publisher Robert Morison who assisted Scott with the description of medieval Perth that forms the backdrop to *The Fair Maid of Perth*.

It is widely believed that Walter Scott made three principal visits to Perth – in 1786, 1793, and 1796 – no conclusive evidence exists, however, to confirm these dates despite their general acceptance. The first of these visits, Scott's boyhood sojourn on horseback to visit Stewart of Invernahyle, provided him with the vision of Perth, the River Tay, and the valley of the Tay (recollected by Scott to have been from the Wicks of Baiglie on the Ochil Hills past Dron Hill) that he used in *The Fair Maid of Perth* – known locally since the publication of *The Fair Maid of Perth* as 'Scott's View'.[1]

Scott's and later generations have mused over whether the passage of time dulled the writer's memory and caused him to describe the incorrect location of his first sight of Perth. James William Jack in his 1933 study, *Scott's view from the Wicks of Baiglie: The roads and the viewpoint*, concluded 'Scott's View' is exactly as described in *The Fair Maid of Perth;* other commentators have argued the contrary.

Following the publication of *The Fair Maid of Perth*, visitors flocked to Perth to see for themselves the setting of the popular novel.

Left—View from St Magdalene's Hill.

CENTRAL PERTH
TOPOLOGICAL MAP

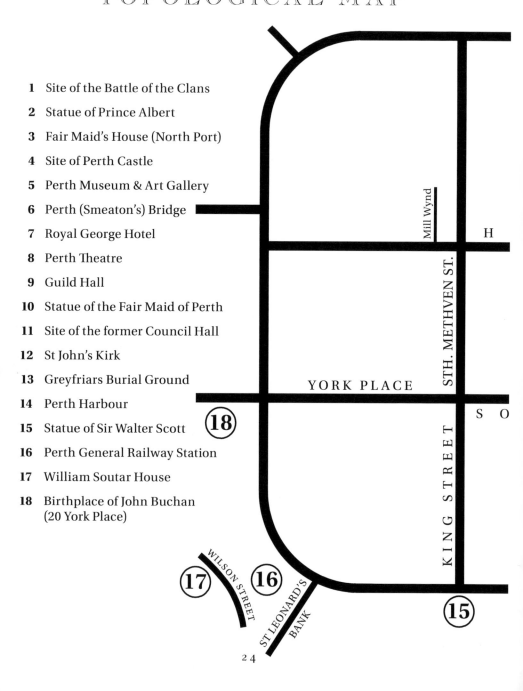

1 Site of the Battle of the Clans

2 Statue of Prince Albert

3 Fair Maid's House (North Port)

4 Site of Perth Castle

5 Perth Museum & Art Gallery

6 Perth (Smeaton's) Bridge

7 Royal George Hotel

8 Perth Theatre

9 Guild Hall

10 Statue of the Fair Maid of Perth

11 Site of the former Council Hall

12 St John's Kirk

13 Greyfriars Burial Ground

14 Perth Harbour

15 Statue of Sir Walter Scott

16 Perth General Railway Station

17 William Soutar House

18 Birthplace of John Buchan
    (20 York Place)

Mill Wynd

STH. METHVEN ST.

H

YORK PLACE

18

S   O

KING STREET

17 WILSON STREET 16

ST LEONARD'S BANK

15

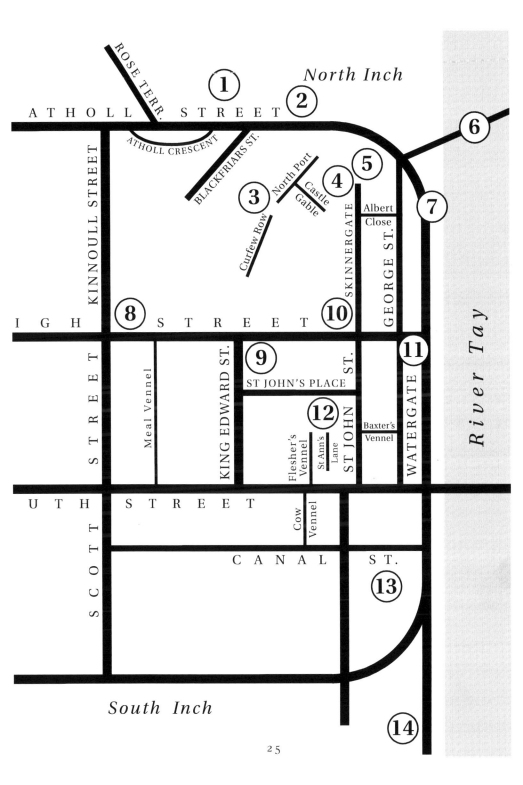

North Inch

ROSE TERR.

ATHOLL STREET

ATHOLL CRESCENT

BLACKFRIARS ST.

KINNOULL STREET

North Port

Castle Gable

Curfew Row

SKINNERGATE

Albert Close

GEORGE ST.

River Tay

IGH STREET

STREET

Meal Vennel

KING EDWARD ST.

ST JOHN'S PLACE

ST. JOHN ST.

WATERGATE

Flesher's Vennel

St Ann's Lane

ST JOHN

Baxter's Vennel

SCOTT STREET

UTH STREET

Cow Vennel

CANAL ST.

South Inch

THE FAIR MAID OF PERTH
& SIR WALTER SCOTT

A Guided Tour

ALBERT CLOSE

Albert Close is an old passageway that runs between George Street and Skinnergate, named after the *Albert Inn* (part of which sat over the close that ran to Skinnergate) – itself associated with the nearby statue of Prince Albert of Saxe-Coburg & Gotha (1819-1861). The 8ft stone sculpture of Prince Albert wearing robes of the Order of the Thistle and holding the plans for Crystal Palace, by William Brodie (1815-1881), (*see also* NORTH INCH), was unveiled by Queen Victoria in 1864. She found disagreement with the form of the nose and so it was re-carved. Until the late 1970s, the people of Perth celebrated annually 'Albert Memorial Inauguration Day'.

A plaque fixed to the wall that stands within *Albert Close* describes the wall as being a portion of old city wall. This is unlikely. The Town Council demolished the city gates in 1764 and two years later removed the last section of the above ground city wall. It is more likely that the foundations of the wall in *Albert Close* formed part of the original medieval city wall thus providing a physical link to the historical setting of *The Fair Maid of Perth*.

ATHOLL CRESCENT

Atholl Crescent is a street development dating from *c.*1795. The laying out of *Atholl Crescent* and its companion Georgian New Town streets in the 1790s was part of the expansion of Perth's perimeter to its north on land close to the North Inch linked to

Left—City Wall Foundations, Albert Close.

then road to Crieff. Many of the *Atholl Crescent* properties retain original features such as Adam-style fireplaces and curved staircases.

Number 5 *Atholl Crescent*, a Georgian property built in 1795, is home to two Masonic lodges: Scoon & Perth, Number 3, and Perth Royal Arch, Number 122. It was acquired for use as a Masonic lodge in 1930. This ornate building fronted by Roman Doric columns includes a rather beautiful Masonic temple dating from 1932 – one of the largest and finest examples of its type in Scotland. On the walls of the temple are four large hand-painted murals by Thomas Hutchison Peddie, (1871-1954) artist and mason. Peddie also painted *The Fair Maid of Perth with the Carthusian Monk* (1895), which is today in the care of Perth Museum & Art Gallery. A stained glass window featuring the crowning of Robert the Bruce, King Robert I of Scotland (1274-1329), is on display in one of the building's social rooms.

Walter Scott was initiated, passed, and raised on 2 March 1801 in Lodge Saint David No. 36, Edinburgh.

ATHOLL STREET

Atholl Street, a section of Perth's Georgian New Town developments, formed upon its construction (*c*.1800-*c*.1823) part of the turnpike road to Crieff.

The first performance in Scotland of a dramatisation of *The Fair Maid of Perth* was that of C. Bass, lessee of the Theatre Royal, *Jamieson's Buildings*, 5-7 Atholl Street, (with 77-79 Kinnoull Street). Built by public subscription, the Theatre Royal opened its doors in August 1820 and closed in 1845. The Italian violin virtuoso Niccolò Paganini (1782-1840) performed at the theatre in 1831.

Bass's production of *The Fair Maid of Perth* ran for nine nights (with a break after the first five) starting on Tuesday, 23 September 1828. It is recorded that a capacity crowd attended the opening night of the play, which was deemed a rip-roaring success. Attempting to see the play, a small boy who clambered onto the roof of the theatre ended up putting his foot through the ceiling's plaster work. Despite the commotion caused by this accident, the play went ahead.

A notable feature of the play was the costume used by the actor Macgregor in his role of *Oliver Proudfute*. The Glover Incorporation of Perth having taken a keen interest in the play, lent the theatre a sword-dance dress identical to that used in a version of the hilt-and-point dance performed (on a special stage set upon the River Tay) before Charles I during his trip to Scotland in 1633 to receive the Crown of Scotland. Perth Museum & Art Gallery is today home to that costume. Made of fawn-coloured silk, the tunic is decorated with trappings of red and green satin and 252 small circular bells arranged into twenty-one sets of twelve bells mounted on leather strips made to affix to various parts of the dancer's body. The costume has been used for royal visitations including the visit of Queen Victoria to Perth in 1842 and the marriage of the Prince of Wales and Princess Alexandra in 1863.

The Convenor's Court of Perth attended the play during its first run, followed by the leadership of the other Perth incorporations. The Convenor's Court, in existence from at least 1365, was a forum for the Perth incorporations through which matters of trade and city governance could be discussed.

Whilst the Theatre Royal production opened a mere four months after the publication of *The Fair Maid of Perth*, it was not the first dramatisation of the novel. Six weeks after coming into print (23 June 1828), *The Fair Maid of Perth* was performed at the Royal Coburg Theatre, London (today the Old Vic).

A modern memorial on *Atholl Street* acknowledges the Battle of the Clans (*see also* NORTH INCH).

BAXTER'S VENNEL

Baxter's Vennel is one of the six medieval Kirk vennels that led to St John's Kirk (*see also* ST JOHN'S PLACE).[2] The designation 'Baxter', an obsolete term for a baker, reveals the history of this

passage that runs from Watergate to St John Street. The Baker
Incorporation of Perth, in operation from at least 1600,
maintained their hall in the vennel.

Members of the incorporation were required to use the mills
of Perth for the grinding of grain. This form of servitude
(thirlage) ensured the continued existence of mills within the
city. A number of granaries were built close to the mills by the
incorporation in the late eighteenth century.

THE WATERGATE

There is an information plaque about the former McEwens of Perth (now Beales), department store, in *Baxter's Vennel*. Before the construction of McEwens, *Baxter's Vennel* included many examples of late medieval type buildings with upper jettied floors.

BLACKFRIARS STREET

Blackfriars Street is a Georgian street, which lies outside Perth's medieval boundary, close to the site of the thirteenth century House of the Black Friars (dedicated to the Virgin Mary and St Dominic), a friary of the Order of St Dominic (founded in 1215). A plaque on the corner of *Blackfriars Street* and Atholl Street recalls the history of the friary.

> *'Near to this spot stood the Blackfriars Monastery founded in 1231 by King Alexander II. From the Monastery gardens, King Robert III viewed the Battle of the Clans fought on the North Inch in 1396. King James I of Scotland (1394-1437) was murdered within the Monastery on 20th February 1437.'*

The story of the king's murder is famous as much for the deed as it is for the fate of the murderers – Robert Stewart (grandson of the Earl of Atholl) and Robert Graham. These men, representatives of a wider group of nobles disaffected by the governmental practice of James I, and concerned for the main-tenance of their power and estates, attacked the royal apartments at the Black Friars Monastery with some 300 men-at-arms. The attack was a stage in an attempted coup d'état.

Legend has it that James I might have made his escape through a privy had it not been blocked up the day before so as to prevent the loss of tennis balls. Unable to complete his escape, the king was cornered, and, after a fight, killed. His tomb lies beneath the Carthusian Charterhouse (*see also* ST LEONARD'S BANK). James's queen, Joan Beaufort, escaped from Perth, formed a regency government that pursued, captured, tortured, and executed her husband's killers and their allies during the civil war that followed.

Considered the most important of Perth's religious houses, the House of the Black Friars, which had been the seat of parliaments and home to the Scottish sovereigns, passed away in 1559.

Surrounding the friary on all sides were gardens extending to the North Inch and encompassing what today is now occupied by the Georgian New Town developments of Atholl Crescent, Atholl Place, *Blackfriars Street*, and Rose Terrace. From the balconies of a summerhouse known as the 'Gilten Arbour', which stood within the friary gardens, King Robert III watched the Battle of the Clans (*see also* NORTH INCH). The 'Gilten Arbour' has been described as being richly decorated in allegorical and astronomical gilt designs symbolising the seasons, the various virtues and vices, and the signs of the Zodiac. Plans existed in 1837 to restore what remained of the friary garden but they did not come to fruition.

Before the establishment of the friary, the most important building in this area had been the castle of Perth, which was frequently used by the Scottish monarchy. The twelfth century earth and timber castle, with origins as early as the sixth century, was besieged *c.*1160 by six Scottish earls (including the Earl of Strathearn), when occupied by Malcolm IV with whom they had disagreement. The earls lifted the siege after the intervention of church leaders. The flood of *c.*1210 destroyed the castle and the lands upon which it stood passed to the Black Friars.

GREYFRIARS BURIAL GROUND

At the eastern end of *Canal Street*, set back from the road, lies Greyfriars Burial Ground encompassing land that formed part of the Observant Franciscan Monastery (dedicated to the Virgin Mary and St Francis) established by Laurence 1st Lord Oliphant in 1460. The Grey Friars, as the Franciscans were known, maintained their friary in Perth until its destruction during the

Protestant Reformation. After the burial grounds around St John's Kirk reached capacity, Greyfriars Burial Ground became the principal cemetery for Perth (1580-1849).

During the English Civil Wars/Wars of the Three Kingdoms of the mid-seventeenth century, Perth was occupied by the army of Oliver Cromwell (1651-2) and the burial ground was ransacked of 200-300 tombstones to provide building materials for the construction of a large military citadel. The citadel, destroyed a few years after its construction, was built on land now occupied by the South Inch car park.

A collection of nationally important headstones dating from the sixteenth century (including the Buchan Stone of 1580) lies in Greyfriars Burial Ground. The last burial in the grounds took place in 1978. Perth & Kinross Council restored the (Historic Environment Scotland) grade A listed cemetery in 1999/2001. The Tay Street entrance to the burial ground is via ornamental metal gates.

It has been suggested that Water Scott sourced names for *The Fair Maid of Perth* from gravestones within the cemetery.

CASTLE GABLE

Castle Gable, which takes its name from the former proximity of the castle of Perth (*see also* BLACKFRIARS STREET), connects Mill Street to the North Port.[3] Many of the properties that once stood in the *Castle Gable* area (north of the Skinnergate) were demolished as part of slum clearances. The land was later used for the construction of Perth Museum & Art Gallery.

In 1824, three separate dye-works existed in *Castle Gable*, all using water sourced from the northern line of Perth Lade: Nether Waulk Mill, Nether Mill, and an oil/lint mill. Archaeological finds in the *Castle Gable* area include a large number of silver and bullion coins (1803).

It is at a house in *Castle Gable* that Sir Walter Scott has the apothecary *Henbane Dwinning* practising his healing arts.

*

THE FAIR MAID'S HOUSE AND PERTH CASTLE

CURFEW ROW

Curfew Row developed as a suburb associated with tanning and malting outside the city defences at a time not much earlier than Scott's setting of *The Fair Maid of Perth* – the first known suburb of any Scottish town or city. Archaeological excavations in 1999 unearthed tanning tanks and ovens. *Curfew Row* is likely to have been more expansive than its current 75 metre length and included the dwellings of many glovers, the Skinners' Yards, and access to the substantial lands beyond the city walls owned by the Glover Incorporation of Perth.

The Glover Incorporation of Perth is known to have existed from at least the twelfth century. In 1485, the Town Council formally ratified the customs of that craft. Glove making in Perth thrived until the late eighteenth century and brought

34

great wealth to the incorporation, which invested its funds in property in and around Perth: Pomarium, St Leonard's, Curfew Row, Soutarhouses, and Tullylumb included. Today, the Glover Incorporation of Perth still exists as an organisation (charitable) though its role in glove making has long passed.

The popular explanation for *Curfew Row*'s name derives from the custom of sounding a curfew in its proximity to secure the city gates at night. No evidence has been found to confirm this story and, given the existence of a curfew bell at St John's Kirk, another one in proximity would seem unlikely. Scott himself provides some evidence of this in *The Fair Maid of Perth*.

'*In the mean time the bell of St John's church alarmed, amongst others, the inhabitants of Curfew Street*'.

Curfew Row as such does not appear in Scott's novel where there is mention of Curfew Street. It is not clear whether today's Curfew Row is the Curfew Street of the novel.

FLESHER'S VENNEL

Flesher's Vennel, which links South Street to South St John's Place (St John's Square), receives its designation from the former meat (later butter and meal) market held in front of St John's Kirk and is associated with the Flesher Incorporation of Perth.

The Thistle Medallion (inscribed '*LRMB*') found at the vennel's northern end is the marriage lintel (in high relief) of Laurence Reid ('*LR*') and his wife ('*MB*'). The lintel is part of Perth's old Mercat Cross, probably taken as a souvenir after its demolition/removal in 1764. For many years, the lintel adorned the now demolished *Caledonian Inn* at the corner of Canal Street and Cow Vennel.

COW VENNEL

Cow Vennel developed as a droving route for cattle between the common grazing-land of the South Inch and the slaughter floors of the Flesh Market. The vennel (known in the past as Cow Row) provided access to the many crowded tenements that sprang up around it. In 1948, a panel believed to be a section of Perth's eighteenth century Mercat Cross was unearthed at the junction of *Cow Vennel* and Canal Street.

GEORGE STREET

George Street, named in honour of King George III (1738-1820), opened in 1771 as a north-south link between Perth Bridge and the commercial properties of the High Street. In 1786, the street was paved with a combination of rock stones, dressed stone, quarry rubble stone, and plainstone slabs. Today, the only original features of George Street exist above the ground-floor level commercial premises that line it.

Number 42 *George Street* is the headquarters of the Guildry Incorporation of Perth. In the medieval period, the Guildry Incorporation maintained trading standards within the royal burgh and ensured that all merchants complied with guildry regulations. This included *'no sale of goods on Sunday'* and *'no hoarding of food during times of famine'*.

The first Dean of Guild was elected in the early fifteenth century to preside over the Guild Court, a mercantile body which dealt with disputes between traders and collected fines for breaches of the trading laws. The Dean was also responsible for implementing Acts of Parliament and other orders from central government as they affected the guilds.

After 1560, the Guildry Incorporation gave active support to the minister at St John's Kirk and contributed to the salary of the church's Reader. They also paid a pension to their Chaplain. Guildry members were expected to play an active role in church life; if they did not they were fined. The Dean of Guild Court later came to deal with matters of neighbourhood and gave power to the magistrates of the burgh to deal with housing issues. The first floor flat at 42 *George Street* is home to the Guildry Incorporation archives; Guild Courts are still held there.

Perth Museum & Art Gallery, at the northern end of *George Street*, is home to a number of acquisitions relating to Sir Walter Scott.

These include the Glover Incorporation of Perth sword-dance dress (*see also* Atholl Street).

After the death of Sir Walter Scott (1832), the Perth Literary & Antiquarian Society, of which Scott was a member, held a dinner in his honour at the *Royal George Hotel*, George Street, Perth (December 1832). At that dinner, it was agreed to raise money by public subscription for the erection of a suitable memorial at Perth Museum: a white marble bust of Sir Walter Scott in his middle years by the Edinburgh sculptor Sir John Steel RSA (1804-1891) carved in 1849. The bas-relief details a scene from *The Fair Maid of Perth*.

In addition, Perth Museum & Art Gallery houses a self-portrait of the Kinclaven, Perthshire, artist Thomas Duncan (1807-1845) ARSA, RSA, and (in 1843) ARA. Duncan was known for his 'colourist' output, Jacobite themes, and work inspired by the writings of Sir Walter Scott.

High Street

Medieval Perth maintained two principal streets: the North Gate or North Street (today simply known as the *High Street*) and the South Gate or South Street (modern day South Street). The similarity of name causes some confusion in *The Fair Maid of Perth*.

North Street ended at the North Shore Harbour with its merchant quays by the River Tay and provided access to many of the Burgh of Perth's key administrative buildings and functions: the chambers of the Lord Provost, the burgh strong-room with its seal, records, and charters, and the city's pillory and Mercat Cross. Destroyed by Cromwellian troops during their occupation of Perth (1651-2), the original Mercat Cross (possibly a small chapel-like construction) sat sandwiched between the Kirkgate (to its south) and the Skinnergate (to its north).

By 1669, the cross had been replaced by one designed by Robert Mylne (Master Mason to the Crown of Scotland) and erected in honour of the coronation of King Charles II. In 1765, it became necessary to remove the Mercat Cross to facilitate the flow of traffic along the *High Street*. The former location of the Mercat Cross is today marked by a circular figure on the pedestrianised street.

A fortified gate, the East Port, guarded the entrance to the *High Street* and access to the timber bridge across the River Tay. The bridge is recorded as swept away by floods in 1621. Close to the gate stood the Chapel of the Virgin (Our Lady's Chapel) linked to the river by a flight of stairs known as Our Lady's Stairs. In near proximity to the Perth & Kinross Council complex at the eastern end (south side) of the *High Street* (where it meets Tay Street), a circular marker in the middle of the carriageway indicates the location of the pillory stone, which was used for punishments in medieval Perth and as late as the end of the eighteenth century. The stone that formed the pillar to which prisoners were attached by irons was removed in 1889 and passed to the safekeeping of Perth Museum & Art Gallery (then the Literary & Antiquarian Society Museum).

On the opposite side of the *High Street* is the former Council Hall. The hall is decorated with seven stained glass painted panels (fronting the *High Street*) depicting the key characters of *The Fair Maid of Perth*: *King Robert III, Simon Glover, Catharine Glover, Henry Gow, Lord Provost Sir Patrick Charteris*, the *Duke of Rothesay*, and *Louise the glee maiden*. The three-light window comprising *Catharine Glover, Simon Glover*, and *Henry Gow* was presented by Lord Provost Charles Graham Sidey, whose daughter Isabella (later Mrs W. G. H. Carmichael of *Bon Accord*, Glasgow Road) sat for the *Fair Maid*; the window comprising *King Robert III* and *Sir Patrick Charteris* was presented by Lord Provost Kirkwood Hewat; the window comprising the *glee maiden* and the *Duke of Rothesay* was presented by Lord Provost Thomas Richardson.

The chamber also includes a stained glass window illustrating Robert the Bruce defeating the English garrison at Perth in 1311. This window was presented by the Pullar family of Perth (owners of J. Pullar & Sons Limited, dyers and dry-cleaners) in memory of Lord Provost John Pullar.

It is in a Council Hall that Scott has *King Robert III* take his conference with *Albany, Douglas, March, Prior Anselm of the Dominicans*, and *Rothesay*. Here on St Valentine's Eve, the deadly feuding of Clan Chattan and Clan Quhele was considered and the plan to end the feud by chivalric combat was agreed.

A bronze statue by Graham Ibbetson of '*The Fair Maid of Perth*' (1992) sits at the eastern end of the High Street. In decades past, the *Rob Roy Inn* traded in the High Street.

At the western end of the *High Street* sits Perth Theatre where in September 1932 the company performed an adaptation of *The Fair Maid of Perth* by William S. Heggie as part of the city's celebration of the centenary of the death of Sir Walter Scott.

Near Perth Theatre, a stainless steel plaque (erected in 2008) marks the spot where the hall of the Hammermen Incorporation of Perth once stood. The incorporation whose motto was '*By Hammer and Hand do all Arts Stand*' included metalworkers (armourers, blacksmiths, brass and iron founders, cutters, goldsmiths, gunsmiths, jewellers, plumbers, silversmiths, tinsmiths, and weapon makers) as well as coach builders, furriers, and harness and saddle makers. A medieval guild, the Hammermen was incorporated in 1518.

A public house known as the *Hammermen Tavern* traded in the *High Street* between 1907 and 1950. A painted stone plaque associated with the tavern, bearing amongst other images a golden anvil, is in the possession of Perth Museum & Art Gallery. Perth's former Guild Hall is situated at Number 102-106 *High Street* and is commemorated by signage.

'The first Guild Hall was built when the ground was purchased in 1722. This hall lasted precariously until 1906, when the Management Committee of the day decided to demolish it and erect a new hall on the site. The foundation stone was laid in

1907 by reigning Dean of Guild James Barlas. The hall was officially opened on 29th August 1908 and it served as the focal point for all the Guild's activities until 1988 when as a result of damage sustained during neighbouring building works the hall was beyond economic repair and it was sold for development.'

The Tailor Incorporation of Perth, which existed from as early as 1525, maintained their hall where Number 227 *High Street* exists today. Comprising two sciences, the tailors and staymakers, the incorporation was financially ruined in the early part of the nineteenth century as a result of the corruption of two boxmasters, which made necessary the sale of the incorporation's property. Despite this setback, the Tailor Incorporation of Perth survived as an organisation until the start of the current century.

KING EDWARD STREET

King Edward Street connects South Street to the High Street. It is from the domination of the street by the City Halls that the earlier name for the street arose, City Hall Square. The street's designation is after King Edward VII (1841-1910), who gave his consent to the naming and whose memorial stands nearby. Laid out in 1901/2, King Edward Street has also been known as West St John Street.

Within the street is the Edward VII Memorial built in 1913 as a replica of Perth's Mercat Cross. The memorial includes the insignia of Perth's guilds, a bronze image of King Edward VII, a unicorn carrying a shield bearing a Saltire, and an inscription.

'In the roundels above are the insignia of the guilds that comprise Perth's Guildry Incorporation: Wrights, Glovers, Weavers, Baxters, Cordiners, Hammermen, Fleshers and Tailors. The shaft of the cross is topped by a unicorn holding a shield, and carrying a bronze flagstaff and saltire'.

*

KING STREET

King Street, laid out in 1803, is today a collage of buildings that range from the eighteenth to the late twentieth century. A begrimed, damaged, and recently repaired freestone statue of Sir Walter Scott (1845) mounted on a square-plan stone plinth is situated at the King Street (northern) entranceway to the South Inch. The grade C listed memorial was made by a local firm of mason sculptors – Cochrane Brothers – who were also responsible for the statue of Lord Provost Hay Marshall of Glenalmond (1768-1808) which forms part of the Perth Museum & Art Gallery building.

THE SIR WALTER SCOTT STATUE, SOUTH INCH

John, James, and David Cochrane were Perth-born artisans who emigrated to Canada in the mid-1840s where they produced marble and stone sculptures of worth. Their *King Street* statue depicts a toga-swathed Sir Walter Scott standing by a broken column; his faithful deerhound Maida by his side. It is inscribed '*Sir Walter Scott Baronet, 1771-1832*'. The statue bought by council authorities for £10 in 1845 stood at the River Tay (eastern) end of the High Street until its relocation to the South Inch in 1877.

KINNOULL HILL

Kinnoull Hill (*c.*222 metres above sea level) lies east of the River Tay close to the centre of Perth. The view from the hill's summit takes in the River Tay and the Carse of Gowrie; a view that has been likened to that of the Rhine Valley.

Scott has *Father Clement* and *Catharine Glover* employ *Kinnoull Hill* as a place for religious discussion and inspiration.

MEAL VENNEL

Meal Vennel was a medieval north-south route way that linked South Street and High Street. The vennel received its designation from its association with an important store for oatmeal and other milled foodstuffs – Perth Meal Girnal – which stood at its northern end. With the construction of St John's Shopping Centre (completed in 1988) the vennel found itself incorporated into the retail complex. Archaeological excavations in 1983 found evidence of medieval metalworking in the vennel.

In *The Fair Maid of Perth*, *Meal Vennel* is home to *Oliver Proudfute*, Scott's unfortunate bonnet maker who, mistaken for *Henry Gow*, is brutally murdered.

MILL WYND

Mill Wynd originated as a medieval route way linking the High Street to the city's mills. During the seventeenth and eighteenth centuries, *Mill Wynd* was associated with a community of Flemish handloom weavers. The modern street was laid out in the 1790s along the western boundary of medieval Perth.

The adjacent South Methven Street includes an access route (pend) to *Mill Wynd*.⁴ It is here that a building used by Scott as the model for the house and workshop of *Henry Gow* (*Hal o' the Wynd*) may be found. The former home and premises of Scott's hero no longer exists. What remains is part of an early eighteenth century Flemish-styled harled mansion altered during the early 1980s. Today, only the gable end of the mansion is visible.

NORTH INCH

In his *The Fair Maid of Perth*, Scott immortalizes an actual historical event recalled as the Battle of the Clans and about which very little is known for certain. The Exchequer Rolls of the time do however detail an expenditure for the construction of a stockade within which a judicial contest took place: expenditure of £14 2s 11d for '*wood, iron, and making the enclosure for sixty persons fighting the Inch of Perth*'. Historical sources disagree as to the battle casualties some suggesting as few as seven survived, others eleven.

In Scott's novel, the battle, a resolution of a long-running feud under the right of judicial combat between Clan Chattan and Clan Quhele, takes place on Palm Sunday, 28 September 1396 within an especially constructed wooden and iron stockade on the *North Inch*. Each clan elected thirty men plus a piper and a standard-bearer to fight without quarter until victorious. *King Robert III* and *Queen Anabella Drummond*, viewed the fight from a nearby garden of the Dominican friary. Clan Chattan was victorious and only one man of Clan Quhele survived. He escaped by swimming across the River Tay.

For many years, a bore stone believed to mark the site of the Battle of the Clans lay in the centre of the *North Inch* directly across from the Old Academy building in Rose Terrace. In all likelihood, the bore stone was a flag base used for the standard of troops mustering or camped on the *North Inch* (in and after the later seventeenth century).

The Battle of the Clans is central to the plot of *The Fair Maid of Perth*, so much so that in an early draft of the novel Scott used the title, *The North Inch of Perth*.

In 1932, as part of the Sir Walter Scott centenary celebrations, a re-enactment of the Battle of the Clans was performed on the *North Inch*. Another re-enactment of the battle took place in June 1949 during a historical pageant at Muirton Park, the cast comprising local drama groups; and the fighters being supplied by soldiers from the Black Watch Regiment barracked in Perth.

NORTH PORT

NORTH PORT
North Port is a medieval street, which today includes buildings that range from the seventeenth century to the present day.

Situated in *North Port* on the corner of Blackfriars Wynd, the Fair Maid's House is the oldest secular building in Perth.

There has been a house on this site since at least as long ago as 1475, in which year it passed into the hands of John and Isabella Frew from the owners of the land, the Dominican friary. The area has long-time and close associations with the Glover Incorporation of Perth and the House bears, on a lintel, the motto of the Incorporation.

'Grace and Peace.'

The precise date on which the Glover Incorporation of Perth acquired what became known as the Glovers' Hall from the successors of the Frew family is unknown, but an examination of the relevant documents reveals that it was at some time between 1619 and 1622. There is some doubt whether the hall used by the Glover Incorporation for the next two centuries is the same building as that which existed in 1475. The likeliest explanation, supported by recent archaeological investigations, is that it had been at least partially reconstructed.

In October 1758, the Glovers received an offer to buy the hall from Lord John Murray (1711-1787), who owned the adjacent property. The sale, however, did not take place; this was also the outcome of a further offer, in 1786, from a Mrs Miller. Although in 1786, the Glover Incorporation had built a new hall in George Street, the old hall remained in their ownership until, when in May 1829, it was purchased by John Miller, a solicitor who had formerly been their Clerk.

After passing, briefly, through the hands of James Condie, another solicitor, it was bought back by the Glovers in 1858 – probably because it had been made famous by Scott's novel. The house was, however, by then in very poor condition – a state from which it was rescued in 1890, when it was again sold, this time to William Japp of Alyth, a solicitor and Perth's Chie Magistrate. Japp set out to rebuild it, his reconstruction being intended to make the house resemble Scott's fictional descriptions and included the enclosing of the original external staircase.

In 1899, the final change of ownership took place when it was sold to the Town Council. Throughout the twentieth century, it was put to a wide variety of purposes until the 2010-11 redevelopment for the Royal Scottish Geographical Society (RSGS), which preserved the historic character of the house and, whilst introducing modern additions, ensured that the Fair Maid's House has a long future. The RSGS development, which is open to visitors, takes in the adjacent Lord John Murray's House. A plaque on that building recalls this history.

'Site of Town House occupied from 1755 to 1787 by
Lord John Murray, M.P. for Perthshire, 1734-81,
and appointed General of H.M. Forces in 1770 A.D.'

LORD JOHN MURRAY'S HOUSE, NORTH PORT

In *The Fair Maid of Perth* the ground floor of the house is occupied by *Simon Glover's* workshop, the floor above provided the living quarters, and above that is the loft where *Conachar* lived.

At one time, a dirling pin, one of two still in existence in Scotland, formed part of the handle of the entrance door to the stairway. It is now in safekeeping.

PERTH BRIDGE

Perth Bridge (also known as Smeaton's Bridge after its designer John Smeaton who is regarded as the father of British civil engineering, and is associated with the third Eddystone lighthouse and the Forth & Clyde Canal) stands at the eastern end of Charlotte Street. The nine-span (seven-arch) 893ft pink sandstone/red ashlar bridge completed in 1772 cost £25,000 to build. The Earl of Kinnoull (with the then Lord Provost, William Stewart – 1758, 1766, and 1780 – in attendance) laid the bridge foundation stone in 1766. Finance for the bridge came partially from state-seized Jacobite estates and partially from the local business community keen to promote communication links and improve the Perth economy.

The bridge followed earlier constructions destroyed by flood: 1209/10, 1589, and 1621 (Robert Mylne's stone bridge built in 1617); and replaced the ferries that connected the banks of the River Tay between 1621 and 1766. The bridge does not follow the same line as these earlier constructions, which were at the end of the High Street.

Within two years of completion, *Perth Bridge* passed a test of its worth in the severe flood of 1774. Notable flood levels are marked on the first pillar on the western bank of the River Tay within the *North Inch*. These include the major floods of 1774, 1814, and 1993. All told since *c.*1210 when the castle of Perth was swept away, around thirty-five floods have been recorded in Perth.

In 1787, the burgh authorities added Huntingtower Quarry whinstone paving to the bridge and in 1859, a tramline for horse-drawn trams. Increased traffic levels/vehicle size necessitated

PERTH (SMEATON'S) BRIDGE

a widening of the *Perth Bridge* in 1869/70, which involved the addition of pedestrian footpaths supported by cast-iron brackets. In addition, a tollhouse was built at the eastern end of the bridge and cast-iron lamps placed along the bridge. In 1905, electric trams were introduced, which operated until 1929.

Originally, the grade A listed bridge featured circular oculi to allow the passage of floodwater but these are now filled. With the establishment of the bridge, the settlement at the eastern end soon became known as Bridgend.

PERTH GENERAL RAILWAY STATION

Perth General Railway Station was built *c*.1849 (architects William Tite and A. & A. Heiton) as a joint venture between the Perth & Dundee Railway, the Scottish Midland Junction Railway, and the Scottish Central Railway. Initial plans placed the station on the South Inch, but after resistance from local residents, the railway companies chose a location adjacent to the inch, acquiring the land from the Glovers Incorporation. For a long period,

Perth General Railway Station operated as a major railway centre and hub. Today, the station operates seven (of its nine) platforms.

It is worth noting that *St Valentine's Day* is the formal name of Scott's Perth-based novel, *The Fair Maid of Perth*, being its other name and that by which it has become popularly known. In 2014, in an attempt to acknowledge this fact and to celebrate Scott's Perthshire legacy, *Made in Perth*, a charity set up to promote arts, heritage, culture, and ideas in Perth, launched an initiative to see to the renaming of *Perth General Railway Station* as *Perth St Valentine*.

Edinburgh Waverley is, it is believed, the only station in the world named after a novel, Perth, it is hoped, could become the second. There is some connection between the two stations. The 2013 film *The Railway Man*, (directed by Jonathan Teplitzky) starring Colin Firth and Nicole Kidman – the story of Eric Lomax, a British army officer tortured in a Japanese military labour camp during the second world war after the fall of Singapore – features a scene set in *Edinburgh Waverley*. Significantly, the scene is filmed at *Perth General Railway Station*: the layout of the station at Perth bearing a close resemblance to that of *Edinburgh Waverley* as it was in the 1980s, with a similar semi-terminal design.

PERTH HARBOUR

Perth Harbour is a 1.2 hectare tidal basin located thirty miles from the open sea and associated with trade from the Baltic, the Low Countries, Scandinavia, and the eastern ports of England. Built in 1840 (Robert Stevenson & Sons), the harbour offers modern port facilities: forty-tonne capacity mobile cranes and 418 metres of quay. The harbour tugboat is named the *Fair Maid of Perth*.

PITCULLEN TERRACE

Scott's aunt (his mother's half-sister), Christian Rutherford (1759-1819), resided at 28 *Pitcullen Terrace*, then latterly in South

Charlotte Street, Edinburgh. 28 *Pitcullen Terrace* remained within the Rutherford family for some years; a William Rutherford, joiner, is listed as residing there as late as 1911.[5]

ST ANN'S LANE

St Ann's Lane is one of the six medieval Kirk vennels that led to St John's Kirk. The vennel runs from South St John's Place to South Street and once provided access to the now demolished Chapel & Hospital of St Ann (and its burial ground). The chapel, which was situated on the eastern side of *St Ann's Lane*, was destroyed in 1559 (*see also* ST JOHN'S PLACE); the hospital survived and continued to operate until 1586.

The Chapel of St Ann, named in honour of the mother of the Virgin Mary, provided part of the site (south-west section of the lane) later built upon to create the pre-Reformation Grammar School of Perth (built *c.*1656 to replace the earlier Speygate/South Street building destroyed by Cromwellian troops in 1651-2). It is for this reason that the vennel became known as School Vennel.

The area around *St Ann's Lane* has been the subject of archaeological activity – especially in the mid-1970s during construction work for a local office of the General Accident, Fire & Life Assurance Corporation, Limited. Several medieval artefacts were recovered from *St Ann's Lane*.

On 22 June 1818, a dramatisation of Scott's novel *Rob Roy* was produced at the Old Grammar School Theatre in *St Ann's Lane* just three months after its first ever production at Covent Garden Royal Theatre, London. The Old Grammar School Theatre operated from 1810 to 1819.

ST JOHN'S PLACE – ST JOHN'S KIRK

St John's Place originally formed part of the city's graveyard until its replacement by Greyfriars Burial Ground in 1580.

St John's Kirk (situated by *St John's Place*) is one of the earliest stone built churches in Scotland and the oldest building in Perth. Archaeological evidence suggests the presence of a church dedicated to St John the Baptist in Perth as early as the end of the tenth century. In 1126, King David I granted the revenues of the church to the Benedictine Abbey of Dunfermline.

ST JOHN'S KIRK

St John's Kirk is the resting place of the heart of King Alexander III (1241-1286) and played a central role in the early part of the Scottish Protestant Reformation. It was here, on 11 May 1559, that the Protestant reformer John Knox (*c*.1505-1572) preached his infamous sermon against idolatry that led to the smashing of the church's altars and the destruction of Perth's religious houses and monasteries.

Scott located the trial by 'Bier Right', the attempt to find the murderer of the bonnet maker *Oliver Proudfute*, in St John's Kirk. In attendance at the trial were *King Robert III* and his court.

Archaeological work within and around *St John's Place* has been very fruitful and includes: a hoard of coins (*c*.1920) and skeletons unearthed during sewer work (1991); and human remains, medieval foundations, wooden flooring, a nineteenth century cellar, and a prehistoric flint scraper during recent restoration work.

ST LEONARD'S BANK

St Leonard's Bank received its name from the medieval Priory, Hospital & Chapel of St Leonard that stood nearby. A plaque at the southern end of *St Leonard's Bank* details the history of this religious house.

'In this vicinity stood the Priory, Hospital & Chapel of St Leonard founded before 1296 *– gifted by James I to the Prior and Convent of the Charterhouse in* 1429 *– suppressed in* 1434.'

The remains of the priory lie below St Leonard's Bridge under the railway sidings (just west of Platform 4). The priory's lands took in Priory Place and ran up to the Craigie Burn. Archaeological finds in this area include human remains, a brooch enclosed in a full size stone cist, medieval pottery, and a portion of daub.

Elizabeth Dunbar, daughter of the *Earl of March*, who appears as a character in *The Fair Maid of Perth* was around the turn of the fourteenth century Prioress of St Leonard's.

SCOTT STREET

Originally laid out in 1803, *Scott Street*, named in honour of Sir Walter Scott, was constructed in the later nineteenth century. The first section, from Canal Street to South Street dates from *c.*1877; the corner block with South Street has a date plaque of 1889. In 1893-5 further work extended the street as New Scott Street to the High Street.

SKINNERGATE

Skinnergate has a name that recalls the long association of Perth with the tanning of animal hides/skins (goats, sheep, cows, calves, cats, and dogs) for use in glove making and other crafts. When the industry was at its height, the Glovers Incorporation of Perth manufactured some 30,000 pairs of gloves annually. By the eighteenth century, the industry was in decline.

During the medieval period, *Skinnergate* became an important route between Castle Gable to its north (until the destruction of Perth Castle by the flood of *c.*1210) and St John's Kirk. *Skinnergate* has been a rich source of archaeology; finds include millstones (1851) and silver coins (1854). In 1991, excavations in *Skinnergate* unearthed a section of Perth's medieval walls.

SOUTH METHVEN STREET

South Methven Street though laid out in 1791 along the western boundary of medieval Perth, presents itself today very much as a modern street with both a residential and commercial profile.

The street was once home to the *Hal o' the Wynd Bar*, a public house adorned with a small statue of Henry Gow, the bare alcove of which remains today.

SOUTH STREET

South Street, originally also known as South Gate was the second main street of medieval Perth. Several narrow vennels maintain communication between High Street and *South Street*. The South Port, which stood at the end of the street, existed until 1774.

The street was known in the medieval period as the Shoe Gait after the shoemakers' market held there every Friday.[6] The Shoemaker Incorporation of Perth, which existed from at least 1545, maintained their hall where Number 97 *South Street* exists today. The incorporation was wound up in 2000.

The Flesher Incorporation of Perth, for which records exist from *c.*1598, operated their hall in *South Street* until the 1920s. A carved relief of the guild's symbol on the late nineteenth century red sandstone building that is Number 46-50 *South Street* memorialises the hall.

Number 103 South Street is traditionally deemed Weaverland Close after the now demolished hall of the Weaver Incorporation of Perth that stood nearby. Records of the incorporation exist from 1671 though the incorporation was active earlier. The incorporation no longer exists.

WATERGATE

Watergate is the oldest street in Perth, being the site of the city's earliest settlements. For many centuries, *Watergate* was one of the principal thoroughfares of the city. It linked St John's Kirk, the High Street, and South Street. Its name, originally, Water Gait, is derived from its proximity to the River Tay. Until the turn of the sixteenth century, the city's nobility and wealthy merchants had their homes here. Today, the earliest surviving buildings date from the eighteenth century.

The Venue (the main entrance of which lies in St John Street) was known in the mid to later nineteenth century as the *Sir Walter Scott Tavern*.

The hereditary Lord High Constable and Knight Marischal of Scotland (the *Earl of Errol*), employed as a character by Scott in *The Fair Maid of Perth* had his home on the western side of the southern end of the *Watergate*.

For more than two centuries, the Wright Incorporation of Perth maintained their hall in *Watergate*. The trades within the Wright Incorporation included barbers, bookbinders, carpenters,

THE WATERGATE

glaziers, masons, and weavers. A wall-mounted plaque provides information as to the history of the incorporation.

> *'Within these premises, 21-29 Watergate, the meetings of The Wright Incorporation of Perth were held from 1725 until 1968, when the building was sold and further developed into flats; it was constructed in 1725 by The Wright Incorporation with a hall and six flats.'*

During the renovations, the interior of the building was completely changed and the spiral staircase that led up to the incorporation's Deacon Court removed.

Number 23 *Watergate* features the ornamental Wrights' Door, a gift to the Wright Incorporation from the Masons' Guild that once used the hall. A number of pieces of furniture belonging to the Wright Incorporation are housed in Perth Museum & Art Gallery.

The Jacobite Army of Prince Charles Edward Stuart (1720-1788) used the Wright's Hall as a hospital during their occupations of Perth in the 1745-6 rising.

WILSON STREET

Wilson Street, named after Lord Provost George Wilson (1890), in the heart of the suburb of Craigie, comprises stone-built nineteenth century properties as well as later constructions. Number 27, *Inglelowe*, (meaning 'Hearth Glow'), known locally as the *Soutar House*, is the former home of the poet William Soutar (*see* William Soutar's *Hal o' the Wynd* – A Poetical Tribute to *The Fair Maid of Perth*).

The house was built by the poet's father, John Soutar, a partner in the building firm of Soutar & McQueen. There is a commemorative bronze plaque to William Soutar on the outside of the building (unveiled in 1958). In 1958, John Soutar willed the house to the people of Perth.

YORK PLACE

Perth & Kinross Archive maintained at the AK Bell Library, *York Place* is home to several acquisitions associated with *The Fair Maid of Perth*. These include materials relating to theatrical productions of *The Fair Maid of Perth* by William C. Heggie (1932) and Ian Watt Smith (1967) – both performed at Perth Theatre.

John Buchan (1875-1940), writer, politician, soldier, and World War One intelligence officer was born at 20 *York Place*, the then Manse of the Knox Free Church, South Street, Perth, on 26 August 1875. There is a commemorative plaque on the front of this villa that acknowledges Buchan's elevation to Baron Tweedsmuir of Elsfield in the County of Oxford before his appointment as the 35th Governor General of Canada.

Buchan admired Sir Walter Scott and there are many elements of commonality between the two writers, the most important of which is the drawing upon the Scottish landscape as the backdrop for their storytelling. As a writer, Buchan penned more than a hundred books. It is for the still popular *The Thirty-nine Steps* and *Greenmantle* that Buchan is best remembered. Buchan penned three books on Scott: *Some Notes on Sir Walter Scott* (1924), *The Man and the Book: Sir Walter Scott* (1925), and a biography published at the centenary of Scott's death, *Sir Walter Scott 1771-1832* (1932) whose preface includes details of Buchan's love of and linkage to Sir Walter Scott.

> *'The centenary of the death of Sir Walter Scott is my excuse for the recutting of some of the lines of Lockhart's imperishable memorial, and for an attempt at a valuation of the man and his work after a lapse of a hundred years. It is a book which I was bound one day or other to write, for I have had the fortune to be born and bred under the shadow of the great tradition.'*

On 29 September 1933, John Buchan was made a Freeman of the City of Perth. At the award ceremony in Perth City Hall, Buchan spoke both of his affection for the place of his birth and for Sir Walter Scott's description of the medieval burgh.

> *'I am one of yourselves… My notion of Perth was drawn wholly from Sir Walter Scott, and it seemed to me a magical place which must confer a unique distinction upon its natives.'*

* * *

WILLIAM SOUTAR'S
Hal o' the Wynd

A Poetical Tribute to Scott's
The Fair Maid of Perth

'Hal o' the Wynd, he taen the field
Alang be the skinklin Tay:
And he hackit doun the men o' Chattan;
Or was it the men o' Kay?
When a' was owre he dichted his blade
And steppit awa richt douce
To draik his drouth in the Skinners' Vennel
At clapperin Clemmy's house.
Hal o' the Wynd had monie a bairn;
And bairns' bairns galore
Wha wud speer about the bloody battle
And what it was fochten for.
"Guid-faith! My dawties I never kent;
But yon was a dirlin day
When I hackit doun the men o' Chattan
Or was it the men o' Kay?"'

POETS ARE DIFFICULT TO COMPARE. Time, culture, context, and ideology defy objective comparison. The views of the reader in relation to the role of poetry and its form equally make it impossible to decide which of several poets is the greater. Despite this factuality, it may be said without fear of falsification that William Soutar, born in Perth on 28 April 1898, is one of Scotland's greatest bards in both the English and Scots medium.

Left—Model for the House and Workshop of Henry Gow (Hal o' the Wynd), Mill Wynd.

Born in sight of the Tay to John Soutar and Margaret Gow Smith, spending his early years in a flat by South Inch Terrace, Perth, then in a cottage near Perth Harbour, and dying within the burgh, made Soutar very much of Perthshire. His early death on 15 October 1943 was due to an illness contracted whilst in the navy.

Soutar was educated at Perth Academy (the old Rose Terrace site).

> '*That was my eighteenth year while yet the shadow of war was unacknowledged. Then I was one of the fleetest at the Academy; one of the strongest; first in my year at most things; I was writing poetry; I was in love; I was popular both in the classroom and the playing field. I never reached this condition of living fullness again except in brief moments.*'

Soutar, after leaving Perth Academy, was conscripted under the 1916 Military Service Act into the Royal Navy and spent the years 1916-18 as a sailor aboard a battleship on the Atlantic and North Sea. A bout of food poisoning that saw him hospitalised in December 1918 led to his contracting a form of spondylitis that through his lifetime would leave him an invalid and finally kill him.[7] Part of the problem during the early stages of the ailment was the failure of medical experts to achieve the correct diagnosis. Soutar was often told that he had rheumatoid arthritis.

Soutar's literary output began whilst he was a student at Edinburgh University and includes ten volumes of poetry published during his lifetime and one posthumously. His style and approach, in his own words, concerned '*all the passions and pains of humanity stark clear from the shadows of individuality*'. Soutar's religious upbringing and his rejection of its traditional forms and conventionality inform Soutar's poetry and prose. Its topics range from comical rhymes for bairns and adults to serious engagement with society, current events, the role of poetry, and his own existence.

Soutar intended to study medicine at Edinburgh but quickly found it uninteresting and began a degree in English literature. His academic life was affected by his illness and dissatisfaction with the Anglo-Saxon dominated syllabus led in part to his failure to achieve higher than a third-class honours degree. After graduation, Soutar's medical condition and deteriorating state left him incapable of employment but ample opportunity to study philosophy, theology, psychology, and literature. He returned to Perth in 1923.

Soutar was a pacifist and this ideological viewpoint can be located in his poetry and prose. He empathised greatly with Wilfred Owen both for his words against war and for his brilliance as a poet.

'A pacifist cannot compromise but must accept that the use of arms is wrong under all conditions.'

In February 1929, a bout of pneumonia preceded a series of difficult and unsuccessful leg operations. From 1930, until his death, William Soutar was confined to bed. Throughout this period, he worked and wrote; and was visited by many people who would influence him and whom he would influence. Most notable was the poet who was leading the renaissance of poetry in the Scots tongue, Hugh MacDiarmid (1892-1978). It would be MacDiarmid who would be the catalyst for Soutar's move from English to Scots within his writing.

Soutar's bedroom was enlarged by his father and the window through which he would gaze upon and lyricise the world was as large as was physically possible to occupy the space available. Although through even this expanded portal William Soutar could only view a garden, he somehow managed to see the world and the diversity which resides within.

*

Soutar's published poetry includes:

Gleanings of an Undergraduate (1923)
Conflict (1931)
Seeds in the Wind (1933)
Poems in Scots (1933)
Riddles in Scots (1937)
In the Time of Tyrants (1939)
The Expectant Silence (1944)
Hal o' the Wynd (1942)

Soutar's *Diaries of a Dying Man*, not published until 1954 and facilitated by Alexander Scott, articulates, from 21 May 1930 onwards, the story of Soutar's decline and eventual death. This collection of his diaries and notes contain insights into Soutar's view of poetry and poets but also into both humanity in the individual form of those who visited his bedside for conversation and the wider social collective. Details of his failing health can be found as well as Soutar's approach to death and hopeful immortality through his writing. Other prose writings consist of journals and thirty-four *Dream* interpretation books. Soutar adopted the unicorn as a symbol for himself and this image was printed onto five of his books of poetry.

By July 1943, the awful infliction that had confined Soutar to bed had taken hold of his lungs. A few months later, he was dead.

> *'Yesterday's experience of coughing for three hours without clearance... was a most wearing one... I can guess that many very unpleasant experiences are awaiting me; and one of the most unfortunate consequences is the loss of time.'*

In 1948, Hugh MacDiarmid put together a final volume of Soutar's work entitled *Collected Poems*, which despite its name was full of unseen material. Much of the last ten years of his productive output was involved with 'whigmaleeries' – poems of humour, imaginativeness, and hyperbole.

Number 27 Wilson Street, the Soutar family home, was gifted to Perth by Soutar's father in his will. It was for many years the residence of Perth & Kinross Council's writer-in-residence – the 'Soutar Fellow'. Former holders of the fellowship include:

Donald Campbell, Ajay Close, John Herdman, Alan Jamieson, Brian McCabe, Carl McDougall, and Raymond Vetese.

Perth's A. K. Bell Library houses a collection of the personal library of William Soutar. These contain his signature and may be viewed on request. Perth High Street is home to a sculpture which features an inscription of Soutar's poem *Nae Day Sae Dark*.

> '*Nae day sae dark; nae wud sae bare;*
> *Nae grund sae stour wi'stane;*
> *But licht comes through; a sang is there;*
> *A glint o' grass is green.*'

At the end of April 1958, to commemorate the 60th anniversary of Soutar's birth, the playwright Robert Kemp opened a Soutar exhibition at Perth Museum & Art Gallery, where a bust of the poet continues to be on view today. In addition, a plaque was unveiled at 27 Wilson Street. There is an extensive Soutar archive at the National Library of Scotland.

* * *

THE FAIR MAID OF PERTH

An 'Original Tweet' Edition

TWEET 1

On Valentine's Eve begins our story of thirteenth century Scotland as told by Walter Scott, The Fair Maid of Perth, published 15th May 1828.

TWEET 2

Perth with regal form of inch & steeple sits within the beauty of a county gabled by plain Lowland & rugged Highland. Here by Tay we begin.

TWEET 3

Fair Maid Kate & father Simon Glover take friary mass where cloaked lord pesters dark-haired beauty to be his Valentine. Denied, he angers.

TWEET 4

Armourer Gow returns with martial tale & marital aim. At Glover home fight ensues as intern draws blade. Foiled by Gow. Kate upset retires.

TWEET 5

Damage repaired Simon persuades Henry Gow o' the Wynd to rest a while and drink his fill. Simon advises Gow as to win the Fair Maid's heart.

TWEET 6

Valentine's morn at Maid's House chain-mailed Henry thwarts Kate's abduction by men unknown. In royal mêlée a hand is lost, severed by Gow.

Left—Scene of the Battle of the Clans (1396), North Inch.

Tweet 7

As men fight, Perth awakes. Kidnappers escape. Henry guards the Maid's House. In slumber, he is kissed by Kate; his Valentine for the year.

Tweet 8

Spurned in favour with enmity of Henry, Conachar leaves his apprenticeship to return to Quhele his Highland clan, whose chief his father is.

Tweet 9

City elders meet. Debate ensues. Bonnet maker Proudfute boasts of part played in fight (a lie). Deputation to Provost Charteris is arranged.

Tweet 10

En route the delegation meets the Devil's Dick (kin to the Black Douglas) who robs Proudfute. At Kinfauns Castle, Charteris agrees to help.

Tweet 11

A royal play unfolds at friary Dominican. Meek Robert III is beset by intrigue as earls of March & Douglas, daughters two, & a prince, plot.

Tweet 12

March's men enter the friary. So too do those of Douglas. A glee maiden/courtesan charms all – Rothesay the prince included. Trouble ensues.

Tweet 13

Rothesay's sport with the glee maiden angers Douglas his father-in-law whose rage falls upon the girl. Henry is royally charged to save her.

Tweet 14

Henry takes the glee maiden to his home where she is placed in his housekeeper's charge. En route, Dwinning the apothecary spots the pair.

Tweet 15

Meanwhile the king, his bro Albany, March, Rothesay, & Prior Anselm talk of the incident with Kate; & a feud between clans Chattan & Quhele.

Tweet 16

On Kinnoull Hill freethinking Fr Clement urges Kate to view Rothesay as suitor. Conachar, now Hector MacIan clan chief, arrives with guards.

Tweet 17

Dwinning attends Ramorny (axed from princely duty) for his loss of hand. Revenge against Gow is plotted. Servant Bonthron agrees to the act.

Tweet 18

Scared by revelry Proudfute seeks refuge in Henry's home. Leaving he borrows armour & mimics Henry's gait. Hit by axe from behind, he dies.

Tweet 19

Rothesay with revellers enter Ramorny's home to discover it was he who lost his hand. Bonthron appears, bloodied with murderous axe in hand.

Tweet 20

With discovery of body believing it is Henry uproar seizes the city-folk who cry St Johnstoun's hunt is up! Proudfute not Henry calms some.

Tweet 21

Proudfute's widow names Henry champion. Ancient rule of 'Bier Right' evoked. Ramorny's menagerie (suspects all) to appear before the corpse.

Tweet 22

With trouble in the Borders and Perth the king agrees that clans Chattan & Quhele will settle their feud by combat: 30 men aside 'til death.

Tweet 23

Ramorny's men come afore the king @ St John's. Bonthron elects combat not 'Bier Right'. Bested by Henry he admits guilt embroiling Rothesay.

Tweet 24

Bonthron is taken away & hanged by the executioner Smotherwell who is secretly in league with Dwinning. Tricks ensure Bonthron's survival.

Tweet 25

Dwinning and others free Bonthron – who has survived the hanging – from the scaffold. He is whisked away to Newburgh under cover of night.

Tweet 26

Accused of acts of heresy, Kate & Simon Glover aided by Provost Charteris travel to Kinfauns where Kate remains. Simon continues to the NW.

Tweet 27

Simon reaches the home of his friend Niel Booshalloch who tells of the death of Clan Quhele's chief and Conachar's ascendency to that title.

Tweet 28

The funeral of the late chief is held at Loch Tay. From a hill, Simon in the company of Fr Clement views the highlanders honour their chief.

Tweet 29

Eachin Hector MacIan is invested as clan chief on the banks of the loch. Simon joins 200 of Clan Quhele's warriors at the celebration feast.

Tweet 30

Simon spends time as a guest of Booshalloch. Eachin enters the Glover's chambers. He confesses cowardice and fear of the coming clan battle.

Tweet 31

As time goes by developments offer fortune to Kate & Simon's predicament. Fr Clement tells Simon that the charge of heresy no longer stands.

Tweet 32

Ramorny's anger spurs revenge. He lures Rothesay to Falkland with claim of frolics with Kate. En route by boat, the glee maiden joins them.

Tweet 33

At Falkland, Rothesay veiled as Lady Majory bids to seduce refuge-seeking Kate. She calms his passion. Drugged by Henbane he falls comatose.

Tweet 34

After claiming Rothesay has an infectious illness, Ramorny & Dwinning take him to a dungeon wherein he is starved. Behind the deed – Albany!

Tweet 35

Kate & the glee maiden captive in the castle become close. Kate hears the truth of Henry. They hear Rothesay's cries via cracks in the wall.

Tweet 36

Glee maiden escapes; warns the Black Douglas who takes the castle. Too late, the prince is dead. Killers caught. Hanged from the battlement.

Tweet 37

Aware of the Duke of Albany's role in the heinous crime, the Douglas concludes it is politic to let the matter be left to God's judgement.

Tweet 38

Henry & Eachin's rivalry grows. Henry sells his best armour to Clan Quhele to ensure his rival's survival; a chance to fight Eachin himself.

Tweet 39

Combat day arrives. Clan Chattan short of a man seeks a volunteer with offer of gold. Henry relishes the chance to face Eachin and accepts.

Tweet 40

Battle begins: bloody and terrible. The warriors of Clan Quhele perish in defence of their chief. At the end Henry & Eachin each other face.

Tweet 41

Fear grips Eachin who flees by hurling himself into the Tay & swimming to safety. Clan Chattan is victorious. Clan Quhele await dissolution.

Tweet 42

At Campsie, Eachin meets Kate who is staying with the Duchess of Rothesay. Overcome by shame, Eachin throws himself into raging cataract.

Tweet 43

The king learns of the death of his son. Henry vows that in future he will only draw his sword to defend Scotland. Kate & Henry marry. Ends.

* * *

NOTES

The superscript figures in the text refer to the notes below:

PAGE 23:

1. J. W. Jack, *Scott's view from the Wicks of Baiglie: The roads and the viewpoint* (Perth: J. W. Jack, 1933).

PAGE 29:

2. Derived from the French word *venelle*, a 'vennel' is a small street.

PAGE 33:

3. A 'port' is an entranceway into medieval Perth.

PAGE 43:

4. A roofed passageway through a building, a 'pend', (usually) provides access to the street for vehicles within a courtyard or inner building. A 'pend's' key feature is that it punctures a hole in a building, which continues above.

PAGE 50:

5. Sourced from *Leslie's Directory for Perth and Perthshire 1911-12* (Perth: Watson & Annandale, 1911).

PAGE 54:

6. A 'gait' or 'gate' is a path, road, or street.

PAGE 60:

7. Spondylitis is a form of ossification of the vertebrae.

* * *

Left—The Carse of Gowrie viewed from Kinnoull Hill.

THE PUBLISHER

Tippermuir Books Ltd (*est.* 2009) is an independent publishing company based in Perth, Scotland.

OTHER TITLES FROM TIPPERMUIR BOOKS

Spanish Thermopylae (Paul S. Philippou, 2009)

Battleground Perthshire
(Paul S. Philippou & Robert A. Hands, 2009)

Perth: Street by Street
(Paul S. Philippou & Roben Antoniewicz, 2012)

Born in Perthshire
(Paul S. Philippou & Robert A. Hands, 2012)

In Spain with Orwell (Christopher Hall, 2013)

Trust (Ajay Close, 2014)

Perth: As Others Saw Us (Donald Paton, 2014)

Love All (Dorothy L. Sayers, 2015)

A Chocolate Soldier (David W. Millar, 2016)

The Early Photographers of Perthshire
(Roben Antoniewicz & Paul S. Philippou, 2016)

Taking Detective Novels Seriously:
The Collected Crime Reviews of Dorothy L. Sayers
(Dorothy L. Sayers and Martin Edwards, 2017)

Walking with Ghosts (Alan J. Laing, 2017)

No Fair City: Dark Tales From Perth's Past
(Gary Knight, 2017)

The Tale o the Wee Mowdie that
wantit tae ken wha keeched on his heid
(Werner Holzwarth and Wolf Erlbruch,
translated by Matthew Mackie, 2017)

Hunters: Wee Stories from the Crescent:
A Reminiscence of Perth's Hunter Crescent
(Anthony Camilleri, 2017)

FORTHCOMING

Flipstones (Jim Mackintosh, 2018)

The Scots Emoji Dictionary (Michael Dempster, 2018)

A Perth & Kinross Miscellany – (Trish Conlon, 2018)

All titles are available from
bookshops and online booksellers.

They can also be purchased directly at
www.tippermuirbooks.co.uk

Tippermuir Books Ltd can be contacted at
mail@tippermuirbooks.co.uk

TIPPERMUIR
· BOOKS LIMITED ·